GETTING STARTED

Photography is amazing – it lets us record everyday moments and turn them into lasting memories. It can also be an expression of emotion: we can capture sadness, love or amusement. Most of all, think of photography as painting with light. We create art when we photograph bursting bubbles, or the blink of an eye.

This book is filled with 10 simple projects to get you inspired about and confident in photography. Each project introduces a different camera technique, such as shutter zoom or varying angles, so your photography skills and know-how will gradually improve. Once you know the techniques, you'll be able to show other people the world through your own eyes!

EQUIPMENT

All you really need to get started with photography is a camera! However, there are other bits and bobs that will be useful when completing the projects in this book. These can all be bought from photographic suppliers online or electrical shops on the high street.

DIGITAL CAMERA OR CAMERA PHONE
A compact digital camera with automatic settings for exposure, or a camera phone.

CAMERA CHARGER OR BATTERY
To keep your camera going!

MEMORY CARD AND CARD READER
Compact cameras use memory cards to store pictures. You need a card reader to be able to transfer the photos to a computer.

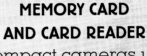

COMPUTER
Computers are essential for editing and storing photos.

RUCKSACK
To carry kit when photographing out and about.

CAMERA CASE
To protect the camera when it is not in use.

MICROFIBRE CLEANING CLOTH
To keep the lens clear of dust.

get into

PHOTOGRAPHY

take brilliant pictures in a flash!

suzie hubbard

WAYLAND

CONTENTS

SETTINGS

These modes are included on all digital cameras. They help you get the best out of your camera by using settings for a certain light condition, or by applying a certain filter. For example, macro mode helps you to photograph objects in focus when they are very close up.

PORTRAIT Takes the strongest shots of people.

MACRO Focuses on objects that are extremely close up, such as insects and flowers.

LANDSCAPE Gets the best out of scenery and outdoor shots in general.

ACTION Ensures the camera does not blur an object that's moving.

KIDS AND PETS Helps to keep wriggling children and animals in focus.

NIGHT Captures the best pictures in low light.

SNOW Shoots snowy scenery in a natural way.

MONOCHROME Records images in black and white.

LONG SHUTTER Keeps the lens open longer, so very dark scenes are given more light.

MINIATURE EFFECT Blurs the top and bottom of the picture.

FISH-EYE EFFECT Takes pictures with a very wide lens, known as a fish-eye lens.

TOY CAMERA EFFECT Darkens the edges of the photo to create a distinctive feel.

SHUTTER BURST Takes lots of pictures very quickly, to increase the likelihood of a good photo of a moving object.

TIPS AND TRICKS

Photography is great because you can do it anywhere and at any time! Your camera can turn into a lifelong friend – and with camera phones, taking photos has never been so easy.

Before we get stuck into our projects, here are 10 tips and tricks to help you start taking great pictures:

1 Remember to switch the camera on – you don't want to see a great photo and then have to spend time finding the 'on' switch, because you may miss the moment.

2 Keep the camera still so the picture does not blur. This is called 'stop-action'.

3 Keep fingers, camera straps and hair away from the lens.

4 Decide whether you want to take a close-up picture by 'zooming in', or take one from far away so everything will appear small and 'zoomed out'.

5 Choose exactly who or what you want in your picture. This is called 'selecting'.

6 Always ask someone if they would like to have their photo taken – and respect their answer if they say no.

Make sure you tell the people in your photographs where they will be featured. Check if they are happy for your photograph to be displayed in public, or posted on social media.

7 Consider how and where you want things to be in the picture. For example, should your friend stand next to a dog or pick the dog up? This is called 'framing', or 'choosing the composition'.

8 Make the picture interesting by trying out different angles, such as taking the photo lying on your tummy or standing on a stool.

9 Check the background to make sure there is no unwanted clutter – and that there are no trees that seem to be growing out of people's heads!

10 Take lots and lots of pictures. The more you take, the better the chance of taking one you love.

PORTRAITS

Portraits are pictures of people, who we call the 'subject' of the photo.

Taking pictures of people isn't just about their appearance – you're trying to get their personality across, too.

First, switch your camera to Portrait mode. This will make the background go out of focus, so it will not compete for attention with the subject.

SETTING

Photographing other people can be quite scary, so why not practise on yourself first? Take a selfie! You can start experimenting without worrying about anyone else.

THINK ABOUT EYE CONTACT
Is the subject looking into the camera or away from it?

SHOOT IN A RELAXED WAY
Don't feel your subject has to pose stiffly. Try and take natural pictures – ask them to move about, use a prop, dance, read or chat to you. It will help their personality to shine through!

FOCUS ON ONE BODY PART

Photographing a person's hands, eyes, mouth or foot can leave a lot to the imagination, but it can reveal something unique, too. For example, everyone moves their hands in a different way. Ask your friends to guess who the subject is based on just one body part!

EXPERIMENT WITH LIGHTING

There are lots of ways to light a picture, and each one gives a different result. Try out light from a window, the sun, the flash of a camera, a torch, a candle and indoor lighting.

HOLD YOUR CAMERA AT DIFFERENT ANGLES

Most portraits are taken with the camera at eye level, but it's worth trying completely different angles, too. Hold the camera up much higher than your head, or down low by your hip, and shoot towards the subject's face.

PAY ATTENTION TO THE BACKGROUND

What is behind the subject? Is it relevant to the picture? A plain wall is good because it isn't distracting – but a lamp post growing out of your head is not a good look!

GROUP PORTRAITS

Organising a group of people to photograph can be tricky. To make sure the subjects don't get bored, why not ask each one to suggest an idea for a photo? It could be making a snake shape of bodies, everyone jumping at the same time, or even a giant group huddle!

FACES
Make sure all the faces in a group can be seen, and that all expressions are captured. Try to get at least one photograph where nobody is blinking!

GET IN CLOSE
Try to get in close to the group, which lets you capture more of the detail in their expressions. This is especially important with small groups – you don't want them to be lost in lots of unnecessary space.

COMPOSITION
A messy image doesn't have much impact. Try lining up your subjects shoulder-to-shoulder, or have some sitting and some standing in rows. Whatever you do, avoid having big gaps between heads – but don't worry about people being different heights.

SETTING

PREPARE

Think about the location of your shoot in advance. Make sure it is interesting and relevant to the group.

HAVE FUN

Look around and see what you can use to unify the group – perhaps pose them on a staircase or under a tree. Or, why not give them some props to make them laugh?

TAKE CONTROL

Do everything you can to make your subjects smile, relax, laugh and talk – bringing them to life will make a better photo. This is called 'building a rapport', and it is a very handy tool when doing portrait photography!

FUN WITH FOOD

LIGHT
Natural light is definitely better than flash. A flash often leaves 'hot spots' on the food, which look like white areas in the images. However, using natural light from a window gives the food a softer and more natural feel.

You can take pictures of a finished meal on a plate, but why not try taking more creative photos as well?

Find colourful foods and break them up. You can even shape them to make an amazing piece of art! It can be oozy, busy, tall, flat, tiny, round or square.

Mealtimes can give us some of our best memories – so don't forget to photograph them!

SETTING

MAKING A PICTURE WITH FOOD
Have fun arranging your food to make an object: perhaps a flower, a pattern, a tower, a face or an animal.

FILL THE FRAME

You are the director of your images: you decide what to put in and what to leave out. Sometimes less is more in photography. Cluttered photos can be confusing, but simple images can really stand out.

BACKGROUND

Try and place the food on a plain-coloured table or piece of card, so the background doesn't distract the eye from the food.

ANGLES

Try photographing food from as many different angles as possible. One of the best angles for impact is from above. You could stand on a chair to help you get the extra height.

ANIMAL ANTICS

It can be very tricky to get good photographs of animals, so patience is important. Focus on what is unique about the subject: ask yourself if it's the dotty markings, white fluff, spikes, droopy ears or tiny feet!

You don't need to photograph the whole animal for people to know what it is – a hint can be very exciting.

GET DOWN TO THEIR LEVEL

Pets' eyes can be very expressive – they are the 'window to the soul' after all! Keep the eyes in focus.

BE POISED FOR ACTION

Animals move quickly when they want to. You need to be patient and then react quickly when something interesting happens.

Set the camera to shutter burst mode to take many pictures quickly. This will make it easier to capture the small movements that an animal makes.

SETTING

NATURAL HABITAT

Capture animals and insects in their natural setting, for example on leaves, in grass or crawling down a branch. It makes the picture feel more authentic.

GIVE YOUR PET A PROP

A ball, soft toy or stick can all encourage the playful nature of animals, especially dogs. It's important to show the personality of the animal – is it shy, noisy, playful or lazy?

DON'T FRIGHTEN THEM

Remember to be quiet and calm so you can get in close without frightening the subject. Don't expect animals to come to you. Avoid using flash – it will scare and startle many animals.

USE TREATS AS BRIBES

If you take some pet treats with you on a photo shoot, you can usually get the animal to focus on their food and stay still!

BLACK AND WHITE

Taking black-and-white photos takes away the distraction of colour, letting you concentrate on the patterns and textures in the photograph.

To understand this, tip a tube of Smarties on to a white plate and photograph them in black and white. The usually bright colours become subtle tones of grey, and you'll notice the shine of light on their shells.

SETTING

WATCH FOR TEXTURE

Photograph different textures to emphasise the shape and form of an object. For example, a brick wall, a driveway and raindrops on a window are all very different!

ZOOM IN

Choose a part of your daily life that usually gets ignored: photograph a section of pavement on the way to school, a pattern on your uniform, or the eyes of your favourite pet.

LOOK FOR PATTERNS

In black and white, patterns often become the most important feature of an object. Once you start looking for patterns, you'll notice them everywhere: cars in a car park, people in a queue or a row of bushes.

COMPOSITION

Keep composition strong by filling the frame with your subject matter and keeping the image simple.

CONTRAST WITH COLOUR

Try photographing objects first in black and white and then in colour. Compare what you find interesting in each of the pictures.

GETTING IN CLOSE

Macro photos are extremely close-up pictures of people or objects. Taking them gives you a chance to explore the world as if you are walking around with a magnifying glass. Stop and explore the veins of a leaf, the spots on a ladybird, or what lives underneath a rock.

COMPOSITION

It's best to keep macro photography simple, so try to remove anything in the composition that might be distracting. You could change your position, move the distraction, move your subject or zoom in even closer to crop the distraction out.

Try getting close up using other modes on your camera too, such as the toy effect or fish-eye lens.

IDENTIFY WHAT INTERESTS YOU

Find something in your frame that will grab the viewer's eye. Think carefully about how to position it.

SETTING

EXPERIMENT WITH ABSTRACTION

Often you can photograph so close to the subject matter that you can no longer tell what the photo is of. This is called abstract photography and is great fun.

LIGHTING

Try not to use flash because it may cause some harsh shadows, taking away the detail of the subject.

LOOK FOR CONTRASTING COLOURS, PATTERNS AND TEXTURES

Getting in extra-close and focusing on part of a flower, tree or rock can create wonderful and unexpected images.

FOCUS IS VITAL

Sharp photography is especially important in macro. After you've identified your point of interest, work hard to ensure it is as sharp as possible. Even a tiny adjustment in where you stand can make the subject matter go out of focus and lose the crucial detail you are trying to capture.

SHADOWS

Shadows can produce beautiful and sometimes spooky shapes, which makes them perfect for creative photography.

Shadows are at their clearest and best when the sun is low in the sky – so first thing in the morning or late in the afternoon. If you're indoors or it is night-time, try making shadows yourself with torches and lamps.

GO SHADOW HUNTING

Once you start looking for shadows, you'll be amazed at all the different types you can find. See if you can spot each shadow from the list below:

- A deep shadow with a defined edge
- A soft shadow with a very subtle, almost feathery edge
- A coloured shadow
- A shadow twisted by the changing shape of the object casting the shadow, such as a tree
- A selfie shadow
- A shadow taken from above
- A line of shadows making a pattern

SETTING

EXPERIMENT WITH SILHOUETTES

A silhouette is the very dark shadow of an object which has a clear outline. To create silhouettes of people, place them in front of the sun when it's low in the sky and point the camera directly at them. The light behind them will create a silhouette.

STAND OUT WITH SHADOWS

For a creative photograph, make the shadow the main focal point of the picture. This could add humour and mystery for the viewer. Which object made the shadow?

To create a shadow, the subject needs to be lit from the side. Overhead lighting or the sun at midday will not do this.

REFLECTIONS

Like shadows, reflections provide a different way of looking at the world around us. They add a depth that is sometimes slightly distorted but very exciting. Remember, on any shiny surface there can be a reflection!

Make it your mission to track down and photograph every different sort of reflection on these two pages.

Never clutter an image with distractions. Only photograph the reflection or the subject being reflected – you don't need to include everything else around you.

WET SURFACES

Rainy days can be the best! Try photographing raindrops, wet pavements and puddles. Water pouring out of a tap or sitting in a sink can also produce magical reflections. Reflections in lakes produce breathtaking results – don't forget to include the sky in the reflections!

MIRRORS

Mirrors have been specifically designed to reflect images, so they're great for isolating your subject and using the mirror as a frame. Include the background around the mirror in your picture to add contrast. Try lining mirrors up so they make an interesting diagonal pattern, such as a series of wing mirrors on cars.

SEEN IN A WINDOW

Capture reflections in windows at home, on a train or in the classroom. Photos can show the actual scene and the reflections in the window at the same time.

METALLIC SURFACES

These produce duller, less clear images of reflections, but they have their own interesting quality. Try scrunching up foil and then flattening it. Photograph the reflections of the light – the patterns can be amazing.

BUBBLES

Trying to photograph the colour reflections in bubbles is a fun challenge because you have to work quickly before they pop! Changing the mode to fish-eye lens will exaggerate the curve of the reflections, producing great results. At Christmas, try photographing the reflections in baubles – these don't pop, so you'll have more time to experiment.

NIGHT GRAFFITI

Night graffiti is when you paint with light at night using torches. You have to use the long shutter mode to capture the result. When you set your camera to this mode, the shutter in front of the lens will be held open for a long time, to allow as much light in as possible. You'll have to keep very still!

GATHER YOUR KIT

Gather a few torches, or other light-emitting devices such as mobile phones or sparklers. To transform plain white light, use coloured transparent plastic to cover your light sources. Sweet wrappers are great for this!

DARKNESS

It needs to be pitch black for the best results.

SETTING

LONG SHUTTER MODE
Set your camera to this mode and select how many seconds you would like the shutter to be open for. If you're just drawing a line in the black sky, a second or two might be enough time, but if you're writing a name you may need longer.

STEADY HANDS
You will need to keep your camera perfectly still during the photograph. If you have a tripod, place your camera on it. Otherwise, rest your camera on a bench or branch – or just hold your breath and try to keep your hands as still as possible!

FOCUS
Preset your focus on the space you're going to photograph: push down the shutter button on your camera halfway for a few seconds so that a green box appears on the back of the viewfinder. This will keep your subject in focus whilst the long exposure takes place.

FRIENDS
Get a bunch of friends together and put them in a line, shoulder to shoulder. Ask each of them to hold a torch, point it at the camera and draw a letter or a symbol.

LIGHT
Aim the light towards your camera as you draw so that the light is bright.

STORYTELLING IN PICTURES

Why not try telling a story in pictures rather than words? This is called 'reportage photography', and it is used every day in magazines, newspapers and on websites to share news worldwide.

You could try documenting something as simple as a walk at the weekend. Plan your story in advance – the story should have a beginning, a middle and an end.

SETTING

1 An 'establishing shot'. This is a picture that sets the scene, letting the viewer know where you are. It is usually a landscape picture.

2 A close-up of you or your friend's feet setting off.

3 A close-up of something fascinating, such as a flower. Gently peel back the petals – perhaps you'll find an insect inside.

4 Look under a rock … what do you find?

5 Who is behind you?

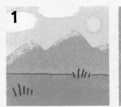 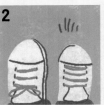 

6 Look up to the sky or to the canopy of a tree, using angles to capture interesting things up high.

7 Can you spot anything funny? Maybe a green grasshopper has leapt on to your arm.

8 Find something beautiful: sun pouring through the leaves, or a glistening spider's web.

9 What's your favourite colour? Find it and photograph it.

10 A final picture. This could be a group photo of smiling faces, or a self-portrait expressing your reactions to the day.

  **5** 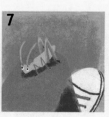 **6**  **7**  **8**  **9**  **10**

PHONE PHOTOGRAPHY

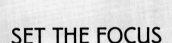

Using phones to take pictures has totally changed photography. Taking a picture is easy, but care and attention are needed to make the photo a good one, just as with other cameras.

SET THE FOCUS

Make sure the subject is in sharp focus by tapping the screen where the subject is. A box will usually flash up to let you know the subject is now in focus.

GET CLOSE TO YOUR SUBJECT

One of the most common mistakes of phone photography is not getting in close enough. Subjects tend to resemble tiny dots in the picture, overshadowed by unnecessary background. Fill up your viewfinder with only what interests you.

DON'T USE THE DIGITAL ZOOM

As tempting as it might be to use the zoom (by pinching or stretching two fingers across the screen), don't! The digital zoom will decrease the quality of your shot and it will end up blurry. Instead, move closer to the subject yourself.

KEEP YOUR LENS CLEAN

Camera phones live in pockets and bags, so keeping the lens clean can be a challenge. From time to time, clean the camera lens using a soft cloth.

KEEP STILL

Keeping your camera still is very important in phone photography, especially in low light or at night. To avoid blurry photos, hold the phone with both hands or rest it on a solid surface.

ALWAYS BE RESPECTFUL

Think about the privacy of friends and strangers when taking photos. Always ask permission to take their photo and tell them how you intend to use the image. Never be sneaky.

EDITING YOUR PHOTOS

Once you have completed some of the projects mentioned in this book, you should have taken hundreds of pictures. However, you'll only want to keep the best ones. Upload the pictures to your computer and take a look!

To start, do a first edit and select your best 20 images. Then do a second edit and pick your best five. Here are some tips to help you choose:

1 Immediately reject anything that does not work because it's too blurry, eyes are closed or it doesn't capture what you were trying to show.

2 Try not to be emotionally attached – what you enjoy taking pictures of won't necessarily turn into the best images.

3 Put similar images side by side on your screen so you can compare them. One might have a cleaner background, a better expression or better lighting.

4 Don't work on the images for too long – have breaks. Looking at images for a long time can make your judgement fuzzy.

Once you have selected your top five photos, you can enhance them with editing software. Adobe Photoshop is excellent, but costs a little bit of money per month. Some free online options are paint.net and befunky.com. You could try:

- Cropping the image, by cutting out the parts of the photograph you find distracting.
- Adjusting the brightness (the overall amount of light in the picture) and contrast (the difference in the amount of light in various parts of the picture).
- Turning the photograph black and white.
- Increasing the colour saturation. This will make colours more dramatic.

The editing process can be very creative, so enjoy it!

GLOSSARY

ABSTRACT PHOTOGRAPHY A type of photography that focuses on shape, form, colour, pattern and texture rather than recognisable objects.

NATURAL LIGHT The light that is present without the use of artificial lighting or flash.

COMPOSITION The arrangement of a photograph's elements, like the subject, foreground and background.

CROPPING Removing part of an image to improve the composition and impact of the picture.

EXPOSURE The amount of light required to produce a good photographic image.

EDITING The process of selecting and altering images.

FLASH A source of light to help illuminate pictures. This is often built into the camera, but can also be bought as a unit by itself.

MACRO Extreme close-up photography, usually of very small subjects.

MONOCHROME Describes something in only one colour, or shades of only one colour.

RAPPORT A good relationship, where people feel happy and relaxed in each other's company.

REPORTAGE From the French word for 'reporting', this means photography that's been captured in 'real time', as an event unfolds.

SELFIE A photograph that you have taken of yourself.

SHUTTER A mechanical part of a camera that opens and closes the lens.

TRIPOD A three-legged stand that helps to keep a camera steady, avoiding blur.

VIEWFINDER A camera feature that allows the photographer to check what will appear in the picture.

WIDE ANGLE A viewpoint that captures a wide scene.

ZOOMING IN Getting a closer view of far-away subjects.

INDEX

Published in Great Britain in 2018
by Wayland

Copyright © Wayland, 2016

All rights reserved.

Editor: Liza Miller
Design: Simon Daley
Illustration: Esther van den Berg
Photography: Shutterbugkids (unless listed
in acknowledgements)

ISBN: 978 07502 9194 1
10 9 8 7 6 5 4 3 2 1

Wayland
An imprint of
Hachette Children's Group
Part of Hodder & Stoughton
Carmelite House
50 Victoria Embankment
London EC4Y 0DZ

An Hachette UK Company

www.hachette.co.uk
www.hachettechildrens.co.uk

Printed in China

The website addresses (URLs) included in this
book were valid at the time of going to press.
However, it is possible that contents or addresses
may have changed since the publication of this
book. No responsibility for any such changes
can be accepted by either the author or the Publisher.

Picture acknowledgements: The Publisher would like to
thank the following for permission to reproduce their
pictures. Via Shutterstock: p 8 Lopolo; p 9 tr Anna
Omelchenko; p9 m Armin Staudt; p 10 William Perugini;
p 11 t Jacob Lund; p 12 kazoka; p 13 tr CroMary; p 13 br
Timolina; p 14 Damien Richard; p 15 tl Jack Hong; p 15 br
Ilaszlo; p 18 Dr.OGA; p 20 Melanie Hobson; p 21 t Sabphoto;
p 21 m Patryk Kosmider; p 22 Undivided; p 23 t Meg
Wallace Photography; p 23 b Cuson; p 24 MaksMaria; p 26
TinnaPong; p 29 Gelner Tivadar.

MIX
Paper from
responsible sources
FSC® C104740
FSC
www.fsc.org